STORY SENSE

for writers

Murray Ewing

Published by Bookship, 2019.

ISBN 978-1-9996269-4-5

Copyright © Murray Ewing 2019.

Cover © Murray Ewing 2019.

Murray Ewing asserts the moral right to be identified as the author of this work.

All rights reserved.

Story Sense for Writers

BOOKSHIP

Contents

Story Sense — 7

Story Ingredients — 11

Character — 13
- Character problem — 14
- Dilemmas — 17
- Some classic dilemmas — 19
- Make them, break them, then break the mould — 21
- Dimension — 23
- Script — 26
- Groups — 28

World — 31
- Rules — 32

Plot — 35
- The Turn — 35
- Acts — 37
- One act, three acts, five acts — 40
- The heroic number — 41
- The classic three act structure — 42
- Stories are fractal — 43

Story Shape **45**

The Hook **47**

The Inciting Incident **51**

The Halfway Point **55**

Crisis **59**

Climax **63**

  The Obligatory Scene 63

  Endings 64

Story Meaning **67**

Story Value **69**

The Vice **73**

Story Types **79**

Some Story Theories & Further Reading **83**

Appendix **87**

The Once Upon a Time Exercise **87**

Bibliography **89**

About the Author **91**

Story Sense

Everyone has a "story sense".

You can tell what type of story you're being told (romance, adventure, comedy, tragedy). You can tell if it ends happily or sadly. You can tell if you like it or not. You know if it *works* as a story.

In the same way that you don't need perfect pitch or a knowledge of music theory to tell a car crash from an orchestral symphony, you don't need an understanding of story structure to appreciate a good story.

But, just as musicians combine their natural, in-born sense of timing, pitch, melody and harmony with a learned knowledge of music theory to further their art, writers and storytellers can combine *their* natural "story sense" with a little learned knowledge to further theirs.

Sometimes, only a little is needed. If you're in the middle of writing a story and feel that something isn't going as well as it should, it helps to at least have the *words* for what it is that needs to be fixed. Or, if you have a great idea for a story, but all it's made up of at the moment is a series of disconnected scenes, it helps to have a basic map of how stories are shaped so you can turn those scenes into a full narrative.

Learning about story structure won't turn you from an intuitive writer into a formulaic machine, any more than learning about sonata form will turn a symphonic composer into a muzak beatbox. In both cases, structure provides a good, solid framework to what they're fleshing out — a basic skeleton to build on, work with or work *against*, to stick to when it's needed or throw away when it's not, to act as a prop when things aren't going well, and to ignore when they're going great.

This book presents some of the basic ideas of story structure. These aren't ideas that tell you what you "can" or "cannot" *do* with a story. They also aren't laws that someone in the past invented and said we all have to follow. They're truths about storytelling that have emerged from the millions, if not billions, of stories we humans have told one another throughout the ages.

They're basic truths we all *know*, and that make up our "story sense", but that we may not know *consciously*. As a writer — someone who works with stories — it helps to have this intuitive knowledge made conscious, so it becomes a tool in the hand, a thing you can pick up and use, or lay aside when you're both-hands busy. But you can only *use* this knowledge, this tool, if you *have* it.

Are we born with our "story sense" or do we acquire it? It's undoubtedly true that we're exposed to thousands of stories growing up, from fairy tales to family anecdotes, television serials to movies, books to comic strips, news items to playground jokes, as well as the founding myths of our many cultures — stories which have actually shaped our world. All that story experience goes into our sense of what makes a story work.

But there's also the idea that stories might be somehow built into us, into our way of thinking and being. Not the individual tales — we don't come into the world with "Cinderella" and "Little Red Riding Hood" imprinted on our DNA, though it may sometimes feel as though they are. But the *essence* of story, the basic map of how a human being is challenged and responds, of how things happen in the world around us, are something that's so deeply a part of us, it *must* have been inborn. It's why we respond to stories in the first place.

Stories mean something because they speak to us at the deepest level. In music, our conscious attention might be caught by the melody played by the clear, high-pitched violins, or sung by a human voice, but at some level we're also hearing the subtler shift of chords below that, the deeper changes going on beneath that melody line. I believe that, in stories, something similar occurs. We read, or watch, or hear them, and are caught up in the actions and words of the characters, the surface details of the world around them, but at a deeper level we're responding to something else, in a wordless way: the ebb and flow of fortunes, the suspense and tension of action, the growth or decline of relationships, and the slow but sure arc of change a story maps out.

Here, then, are some keys to understanding that deeper level: the structure of stories, and how that structure helps the stories we tell work better and be more meaningful.

Story Ingredients

Character

When creating a story, which comes first, character or plot?

Some people say you should start with your characters, others say you should start with a plot. Which is it?

If you have a *story* you want to tell, you need *characters* in order to tell it. What those characters want, what they do, how they react, are all factors that drive your story forward. No story can exist without characters.

If you have *characters* you want to write about, they'll need a *story* through which they reveal themselves and change. They will *want* things, they will *do* things, they will *react* to one another. Without a story, character remains untested and hidden.

So it seems that the best answer to, "Which comes first, story or character?" is "*A bit of both.*" And the further you go along, developing your characters and story, the more you'll find it impossible to separate the two.

There are a two types of stories where this *might* not be the case.

If you're writing a story entirely driven by action, you might want your characters to be just *people who do things*, and who do those things because it's *just what they do*: a police detective solves crimes because she or he is paid to; a soldier fights in a war because that's his or her job.

If you're writing a character study, on the other hand, you might want the story to be minimal, to better focus on your character's inner life: the portrait of an ageing academic writer facing their mortality, a young person daunted by the myriad challenges and responsibilities of coming of age in the modern world.

But even in these cases, both story and character would be markedly improved by having them fit a little better together. You've surely heard the phrase, "This time, it's personal." That means, yes, the police detective *is* solving a crime because that's his or her job, but they also have something personal invested: the victim was a friend of theirs, the killer is someone they previously failed to catch, and so on. And that really adds something to the story.

Similarly, the thing that really brings a character study to life is when that character is faced with a situation which perfectly brings out the best and worst of them, or that tests them to the core — a situation not of their own devising, but which they are forced to face anyway.

Whichever you start with — story or character — is likely to be a matter of how you got your idea in the first place. Pretty soon, you'll be moving between story and character, deepening your characters, then thickening your plot; or exploring your plot, then seeing how your characters react.

How, then, do you wed a character to a story? How do you make it "personal"? The following sections are about the key ways character and story interact.

Character problem

Every character is a story in waiting.

Just as an acorn, given the right soil, sun and water, will grow into an oak tree, so a character, given the right conditions, will reveal something *vital* and *living* about themselves: their strengths, their weaknesses (most often both at the same time), the things that make them who they are.

But while the best way to nurture an acorn into an oak is

to provide it nothing but positive things (sun, soil, water), with characters it's different. The soil a character grows in is *drama*, and drama is all about conflict.

And not just any conflict. Every character has a *perfect* conflict that will bring out their particular depths, strengths, and weaknesses. It's like the perfect conditions that start an acorn growing. The acorn remains dormant throughout winter, while the days are too cold and the soil is too hard, but once the sun warms up and the ground thaws, something inside it begins to respond. It cracks its outer shell and pokes a delicate, vulnerable shoot into the world.

What does the same for a character? What are a character's "perfect conditions", in terms of drama?

Think about what causes an acorn to start growing: a hint of sun, and some good soil. In character terms, "a hint of sun" is something the character *wants*. It might be the pretty or handsome face of a new love-partner; it might be the challenging case that will *really* make their name; it might be the chance of a quick and easy revenge; it might be the opportunity to show off, or earn some easy money, or get famous.

The "good soil", on the other hand, is something the character *needs*, and though it might sound strange at first, what a character *needs* will not be the same as what they *want*. This is where the meat of the drama lies.

That character who sees a pretty or handsome face and moves in with a chat-up line might be *wanting* an easy conquest, but what they *need*, deep down, is love. That's what they're really looking for, but they can't bring themselves to admit it.

That character who takes on the challenging case that will make their name will *want* things to go smoothly, but of course nobody makes their name from doing something that's easy. What they *need* is a real challenge that *proves* they deserve to make their name, a challenge that will take them to the very edge of their abilities, and perhaps beyond.

Sometimes, wants are the opposite of needs. That character who sees the chance of a quick and easy revenge, might *want* to come out of it feeling they've righted a past wrong, but they'll most likely find that things are a lot more complicated. Revenge doesn't satisfy, or it's not possible to simply walk away from it. They might find, then, that what they really *need* is to discover a new sense of justice, or face a much wider sense of wrongness in the world; or perhaps they need to realise that revenge gets you nowhere, and it's better to move on. They might find that what they *need* is not to take revenge at all, but the ability to forgive.

What "character problem" (as a character's dramatic potential is often called) comes down to is the clash between a character's *conscious desires* (what they think they *want*) and their *unconscious need* (what's *really* good for them).

If you went up to your character and asked them what they needed, they'd just tell you what they wanted. But step back, think about it, weigh them up and give them your fullest understanding, and you'd know what they really, genuinely need.

Characters, like all of us, go for the *easy thing* — but what they really *need* is the difficult thing, because it's more satisfying, and more true, and much, much more valuable. Love, not simply a conquest. Self-worth, not simply another notch on your career-belt. Justice, not revenge. Truth, not mere satisfaction.

All this leaves the question, "Why *aren't* conscious desires the same thing as unconscious needs?"

Why doesn't that character who goes for the pretty or handsome face think, "This time, it's love"? Because love is difficult, it involves vulnerability. Merely thinking "this time, it's love", is opening them up to a whole world of potential hurt. So they kid themselves that they're not after love, or perhaps they've given up on love entirely and think the best they can get is that pretty/handsome face.

And why doesn't that character who's offered the chance of that reputation-making case immediately snap it up? Because they *know* they will be sorely tested, and if they fail, they won't just be back to where they were, they may actually lose everything: name, reputation, job, perhaps even their life.

The barrier between conscious desire and unconscious need is *risk*.

Every character is faced with a genuine, testing *risk*. It's what, so far in their lives, has been stopping them from getting what they *need*, and settling for what they *want*.

But this is their *story*, now, and we're going to see them *forced* to go for what they need, and face the risk head on.

That's what makes it their story.

Dilemmas

"Character", in the old sense of the word, meaning not *a person in a story* but the inner quality that sets them apart from their fellows, is revealed by what someone does when faced with a dilemma.

A dilemma isn't simply a choice. It's a non-black-or-white choice, between two alternatives, neither of which is entirely good. It's not a win-or-lose decision, but a decision of what you're *willing* to lose.

Characters going through their daily lives make decisions all the time. Passing the office water-cooler, should they have a drink? Whether they do or they don't doesn't really tell us anything (unless they're on the way to a difficult meeting, and we see their hand shake as they drink).

At the water-cooler, let's say there are some donuts.

Should they eat one? If they do, we're only going to feel we're learning about our character if it's already been established they're meant to be on a diet.

But a little bit away from the water-cooler, two people are having a hushed discussion, and our character can just hear what they're saying. It turns out someone at the firm isn't doing so well at their job, and is likely to be fired. If they *are* fired, someone else is going to be up for promotion. So, these two people are saying, if they put in some extra work for the next month or so, making their own figures look good, they'll be ready when the promotion comes up.

Our character, hearing this, might decide to do the same. A promotion would be good, and yes, it might be at someone else's expense, but if they're not doing their job…

But what if the person likely to be fired is a friend of our character? What if the choice is between loyalty to that friend (warning them they're likely to be fired, and giving them a chance to prevent it) or staying quiet and getting a chance at a promotion? After all, the friend would never know…

You can immediately see that, what our character does when faced with this sort of dilemma will say a whole lot about them that eating-or-not-eating a donut doesn't.

A character's character problem will be the most difficult dilemma they face throughout the story. But they'll likely be faced with other dilemmas on the way. Most of these will have the same "flavour" as their character-problem dilemma, letting us know the sort of strengths and weaknesses our character has. In fact, it can be good to have a character face a lesser version of their character-problem dilemma early on, and have them make the *wrong choice*, to better set them up for their final, make-or-break decision at the end of the story. That way, we know there's a real risk they might fail. (And we'll also know how they *learned* to make the right choice.)

Another use for dilemmas is to make a character a little more admirable in our eyes by, early on, having them faced with a dilemma that tests them just a little bit, and in which they make the *right* choice.

For instance, a cop catches a shoplifting teen. It's an easy arrest and she can bring this criminal in as one more successful arrest on her record. But it's obvious this kid is stealing just to impress some bad older kids he's fallen in with. So, instead of hauling him into the station, our cop says, "This is your wake-up call. I'm giving you a chance to make it good and turn yourself around. We're going to take the goods back to the store, and you're going to apologise. But next time I won't be so lenient."

This obviously isn't a character-problem level dilemma, but it does tell us a lot about our character, and is perfect for setting her up at the start of a story: she's tough (she caught the shoplifter), but she's not going to stick to the rules simply for the sake of it. And we can probably guess that the story to come will be about a similar sort of dilemma, but in which the stakes are a *lot* higher.

Some classic dilemmas

Dilemmas are classic "What would *you* do?" situations, and the point about them is that there's no right answer.

Consider this situation. You and a friend burgle a jewellery store. You get away with a million in jewels but, knowing the police are after you, bury it. The next day, you're both hauled in by the cops and taken to separate cells. There, you're given a choice. The police simply want *an* arrest, and if you confess and implicate your friend, you'll be allowed to walk free while your friend does ten years in jail. But you're smart. You know they're giving the exact same choice, at that very moment, to your friend in another cell. And if your friend confesses, and implicates you, then *they* will get to walk free, and *you'll* be doing ten years. You can also be sure that if you *both* confess, the police will put you *both* away, and probably for even longer, maybe fifteen years. But if, on the other hand, you both stay quiet, you know the cops will only be able to come up with something like obstruction of justice, and put you away for a year or two at most. But if *you* decide to stay quiet, can you trust your friend to do the same?

That's four possible outcomes (walk away, two years, ten years, fifteen years), but you only have two possible actions (to confess, or to keep quiet). What you decide to do says a lot about how much you're willing to sell out your colleague, but also how much you trust him or her.

This is a classic dilemma known as the Prisoner's Dilemma, one of several that have been identified by the field of Game Theory. (Which isn't about playing games in the traditional sense. Game Theory is about working out what to do in situations where you can't be sure of the outcome. One of its earliest applications was in deciding how to act in a nuclear war.) Look up a book or article on Game Theory for some more examples.

Philosophy, in particular ethics, looks at other kinds of dilemma, to determine if there can be a guiding moral principle, a *right* thing to do. In one classic example, you are driving a heavy vehicle when you realise the brakes have failed, and there's nothing to prevent you from crashing. You have a choice, but it's not a good one. You can let the vehicle smash into the car in front, which will probably be enough to stop you, but the car has a "Baby on Board" sticker in the back window. Or, you could swerve off the road and smash into a road-sign in the hope that will stop you, but there's an old couple, a man and a woman in their nineties, in the way. Either way, you're going to end up hurting someone pretty bad, and probably killing them. Is it "better" to risk injuring the old couple, as they're old, and thus save the baby; or is it "better" to risk injuring the baby, who might have better powers of recovery, being younger, but might receive an injury that could last a whole lifetime?

Obviously, it's a horrible situation to think about. But that's the point about dilemmas.

Make them, break them, then break the mould

Here's another way to approach a character's story:

Make them, break them, then *break the mould.*

"Make them" means making the character look good in our eyes. It means introducing them to us in a way that makes us admire them, or want to know them, or want to identify with them. They might do something admirable and be humble about it; they might be kind to someone who's in need; they might prove themselves to be exceptionally skilled or knowledgeable; or we might be invited to sympathise with them for their bad fortune (in fairy tales, they might be an orphan). It only takes a single scene to "make" a character in this way.

"Break them" means testing them beyond their normal bounds. If our main character is a police detective, we're going to assume they're used to solving crimes, so it will have to take an exceptionally bad or difficult case to break them, and that's the case we want to see. If our main character is, as in Jane Austen's **Emma**, a clever young woman who loves arranging marriages for everyone else, we want to see the time when she's caught out — because *she's* the one who has fallen in love and she doesn't know what to do. Her cleverness (the thing that "made her" in our eyes in the first place) isn't going to help her out this time.

Finally, the character has to "break the mould". They have to do something exceptional, both by their own standards and by ours. When they were "made" in our eyes, it was through some display of skill or heroism or character that we were ready to admire and accept. That was the best thing about them, under *normal* circumstances. Now, we've seen them "broken" by *abnormal* circumstances and we want to see their true mettle, what they're really made of. This is where they exceed our expectations, and their own. They go where they've never been before, perhaps where no one's ever been before. They "break the mould".

In the 2013 movie **Gravity**, Doctor Ryan Stone (Sandra Bullock's character) initially earns our respect because of her expertise. Although she's dismissive about it, astronaut Matt Kowalski (George Clooney) points out that she's been brought up into space because she's the only one who can do what she does. This is what initially *makes* the character in our eyes. It's worth our while investing in her, as a character.

Then the story does its best to *break* her. We know she doesn't like being in space, so now she's introduced to the worst aspects of it: she's sent hurtling off without a tether, panicking and unable to even say where she is. The story is now throwing the sort of stuff at her that's perfectly designed to test all her weaknesses and undermine her strengths.

Later, a point comes in the story where she's *utterly* broken. She's on her own, with nobody to help her. Despite her own expectations, she's managed to reach another space station, survive another onslaught of space-debris, enter the Soyuz craft and even remember how to operate it. There's a feeling, at this point, that she's done far more than we ever expected her to do. But the story throws *yet more* at her: the

Soyuz craft has no fuel. And it's just one thing too many. We feel she's quite entitled at this point to give up. And, at first, she does just that. She's utterly broken. But then she has one more try. And this is when, instead of *being broken*, she *breaks the mould*. She goes beyond what anyone could expect of themselves or of her.

Dimension

You've no doubt heard characters in books and movies being described as "three dimensional" (if they feel like real people) or "flat" (if they don't). But what does this actually mean?

In his book **Aspects of the Novel**, E M Forster came up with one way of thinking about it. With him, characters were either "flat" or "rounded" (his term for three-dimensional):

> The test of a round character is whether it is capable of surprising in a convincing way. If it never surprises, it is flat. If it does not convince, it is flat pretending to be round.

Another take comes from Robert McKee, in his movie-writing bible **Story**, who says that "dimension" means "inner contradiction". So, a character isn't only ever gung-ho and positive, but has moments of negativity; they're not only ever strong, but have moments of fear and weakness. Inner conflict is something we've already touched on in our section on Character Problem: inner conflict is the thing that separates a character's *conscious desire* from their *unconscious need*.

Another way to think of it is, three-dimensional characters have *layers*.

Picture your character interacting with different types of people. First, someone they've just met, or know only superficially. A colleague from a different branch of the same firm, for instance. Let's say they go out for a business lunch. Talk is light, and though it may touch on family, it's unlikely to delve deep, or go anywhere dark. Here, our main character is presenting a social façade, their *persona* — a sort of mask or act we put on with most people, a likeable and relatable version of ourselves, keeping worries, insecurities, self-doubts, fears, and all the more difficult parts of being human out of sight.

Next, our main character leaves work and, instead of going home, visits a local bar. They often go there. They're known by the staff and regulars, and consider some of the people they meet there to be long-time friends. Our character bumps into one such friend. Their conversation is likely to go deeper than at the business lunch. After all, these two people have known each other some time. When they talk about one another's home life, they know what's going on, and what has happened in the past. Difficulties might be referred to, but not dwelled on. "Ah, you know how things are…" "Yeah…" Seeing our character in this situation, we get a little deeper, find out more what they're really like, but we know we're not seeing the deepest.

Now, we follow them home. With their family, our character might be quite different. They may even act the opposite of how they were at work. Warm and loving, where before they were superficial; or perhaps angry, taking out the day's frustrations as they can't with work colleagues; or perhaps, at home, things are difficult — there are tense silences, words are few, but laden with emotion.

And perhaps we'll have one more layer. Our main character, having greeted their spouse, goes to their daughter's bedroom. The child is seriously ill. Whatever the day's frustrations, whatever the latest spousal argument, all that is dropped for something yet more fundamental to who they are. Our main character's deepest hopes and fears are tied up with the health and wellbeing of their child. This isn't about what happens in the day, it's about a relationship that has lasted a lifetime, and means everything.

One-dimensional characters will have only one layer. A heroic character in an action movie may be tough and stoic when we first meet them, and remain tough and stoic through every scene that follows, even when they're sorely tested.

A two dimensional character may be bubbly and cheerful when we first meet them, but when things in the story get tough, they may prove to have an unexpected reservoir of strength. This is perfect for a secondary character, a friend or companion to our main character who comes through for them in their darkest moment.

Having "three dimensions" or being "fully rounded" doesn't necessarily mean our main character has to have *three* layers, three different personalities they present to the world. But, when you consider that many stories have three acts (see the section on Acts for more about this), you'll see how this might happen quite naturally as your story progresses.

When we first meet our main character, they're in their normal day-to-day world and doing fine. That's the first layer.

Once the story really kicks off, we'll get to see a new side of them: more determined perhaps, or more frightened, certainly more tested. We'll see how they act under pressure, or when they're in need.

As the story takes a further turn for the worst, or becomes more demanding, and tests them beyond the bounds they've ever been before, we get to see what we might think of as their "true" character: what they're like in situations they've never experienced before, what they're like when they're really faced with losing everything, or gaining everything, or when they're up against death, or the unknown, or the chance of true love, and so on.

Dimension is something that comes out naturally as characters move through a story. Each new step forward peels off another layer, revealing something raw and more vulnerable and more genuine-feeling underneath.

Script

Characters in your story don't exist simply to do what you want them to do. This is one of the things that gives them dimension. They will have their own goals, needs and wants, and though these may eventually align with those of your story, at the start, a character will be busy living their own life, not sitting around waiting for your story to start.

People in stories don't *know* they're in stories. They, like the rest of us, are just going about their daily lives. They have their own wishes, wants, needs, aims, and desires — their own "script".

If your story ends up with your main character saving the world, it's unlikely they'll begin the novel or movie *planning* to save the world. They may daydream about it (we all do that), but when it comes to actually *doing* it, they're most likely to back off. Saving the world isn't in their *script* — surviving, or having an easy life, or saving up enough to buy a new car, or simply getting through a difficult day, is more likely to be their "script". Saving the world can wait for tomorrow, or for someone else better qualified.

Minor characters will also have their own "script". In *their* minds, they don't exist just to serve the story, or do what the main character wants them to do. They've got their *own* thing to do, and that just makes them — and the story — more interesting. If your main character (a detective) turns up to ask them about something in their past, they're not going to say, "Sure, I'll tell you all about it." They might be guarded, or suspicious, or just busy doing other things. Our main character will have to *work* for an answer, and that will turn this from an exposition scene to one where there's some drama.

In any scene, it makes things more interesting if the characters who are talking, or interacting, aren't just ushering the story along, but are questioning each other, reacting against how things are going, or just plain being difficult.

Another danger is if you have a secondary or minor character who is a *type*: a cop, a librarian, a hoodlum. That's okay for one scene, but if they're going to stick around any longer, it's worth fleshing them out. The priest our main character turns to for advice needn't just be a man in a church, he might have a history, experiences, he might have secrets. He can still give the same advice, but it could come out with a little character or colour. He may surprise us into seeing him as more than just "a priest".

This is also true of villains. You need someone for your main character to go up against, and in your story world it's plain they're *evil*. But everyone is the hero of their own story, and your villain is unlikely to have sat in school thinking, "When I grow up, I'm going to be a villain!"

Take a moment or two to think about the world from your various characters' points of view, see it how *they* see it, and try to work out what they want from it. That way they won't just be a *type*, and they won't just be serving the story.

Groups

If your story is about a group of people, be it a family, a superhero team, the crew of a spaceship, or people who work together in the same factory or office, it's possible for the group *itself* to act like a character, having its own character problem, facing group dilemmas, and so on.

Obviously the sort of "character problem" a group faces won't be the same as a single person faces. A group can't fall in love, but it can suffer loss, or disunity, or adversity. Stories about groups of characters are essentially about families. Even if not related by blood, the characters in a group have a reason to be together (work, a shared goal, and so on), that will *keep* them together despite differences, individual highs and lows, scrambles for precedence, and so on. It can be these internal tensions that form the group's story, or it can be adversity from the outside. Often, it will be both.

Sometimes, particularly in action stories or comedies, the individual members of a group might not even have much of a character story themselves, and the group itself is the only thing that undergoes challenge and change.

An example of this is **Ghostbusters**. Egon, Ray, Venkman and Winston don't really change much during their adventures. Throughout, Venkman remains cynical and unimpressed, Egon serious, Ray childishly enthusiastic, and Winston down-to-earth. This happens quite often with comic characters, who can be one-note personalities, walking jokes who keep our interest by being placed in different situations (or always ending up in the same one). But the team as a whole faces being disbanded (when the university cuts their funding), makes a joint decision (to go it alone), experiences success, then failure (when they're all thrown in jail), and then finally redemption as they save the world. The individual characters stay basically the same, but the group goes through its own "character" story.

World

The world your story is set in isn't just scenery. It creates the environment in which your story plays out — and not just a *physical* environment.

It can, for instance, create a *moral* environment. Is your story set in a historical period when slavery was legal? When women didn't have the vote? When the children of poor families were sent out to work? Is it set at a time before there were written laws?

It can create an *emotional* environment. By taking place in an orphanage, for instance, your story will set an immediate emotional tone. Stories set in wartime instantly heighten the emotional stakes around human relationships that could, at any moment, be cut short. Others bring out different sets of emotional values: a hospice, a safe house, a tough neighbourhood.

Certain environments are fraught with peril and bring the basic value of *survival* to the fore: space, the depths of the ocean, the heights of a mountain, the trenches of World War II. Others highlight the need for social virtues, such as *wittiness* (the Court of Louis XIV in 18th Century France), or *social propriety* (the drawing rooms of Jane Austen's England), or the need to obey a strict *social code* (chivalry in medieval Europe, Bushido among the Samurai of medieval Japan).

And it doesn't just have to be a historical period or geographical location that determines your story's world. Stories can be set in areas of the modern world that have their own specific character, tone, and milieu: a story about a legal team will take place in the legal "world"; a story whose main characters all suffer from a particular medical condition will be in a quite different sort of "world".

Your story's world can create expectations, set an emotional tone, and bring to the fore your story's core values. And because it is an environment, the values it brings to your story are both subtle and profound: they speak to the reader or viewer without things having to be stated explicitly. We all know that humans cannot survive in space without a spacesuit, so the sight of an air tank's gauge reading close to zero says a lot without it having to be spelled out.

A good story world comes with suspense, expectation, and an emotional atmosphere built in. Think about what your story world contributes to your story, and make it work for you.

Rules

Worlds come with rules, and rules are important in stories, because they tell us what to expect.

Science fiction and fantasy writers are familiar with this idea. You establish your rules early on — the existence of faster-than-light space travel, for instance, or the fact that casting a magic spell makes you age a little bit — then stick to them, otherwise your reader knows you're cheating.

But it's not just science fictional or fantastic worlds that have rules. All story worlds have rules.

Every historical era, for instance, comes with its own set of *social rules*, some of which can be used to highlight emotional tones and basic human values. Victorian England and 1950s America were both times when presenting the correct social façade was important, and this can highlight the vulnerability of stories about love, or isolation, or being different from the social norm.

As well as social rules, there are actual laws. At times in the past, slavery has been legal, and various groups of people have had fewer (or no) legal rights. Some of the most moving stories have been told around moments when laws are forced to change in the face of a greater moral imperative. But in order for these stories to work, the world's existing laws have to be established right from the start. This sets these stories up to be about not just saving one person's freedom, but changing the world.

Characters can occupy "worlds" with rules which don't affect the entire world, but just them, or a group of people to which they belong. For instance, a protagonist whose legs are paralysed, or who is blind, or who has an overwhelming fear of heights, all come with rules attached, rules which define their story. Someone with diabetes may always need an insulin injection available; someone with agoraphobia may never leave the house.

There are professional rules, or rules of particular areas of endeavour in a world. For instance, if a character is a doctor or lawyer, they will have to abide by the rules of the medical or legal professions to which they belong. If a character works in a royal court, they will most likely have to obey very strict rules of etiquette which make no sense in the outside world. The way things work in a courtroom or royal court aren't as binding as the laws of physics, but any lawyer or courtier who doesn't obey them is likely to get thrown out.

The start of a story can be all about learning new rules. A young soldier arriving at a battlefront for the first time will have a lot to learn, as will the same soldier returning from the front with post-traumatic stress disorder. To both, the world they find themselves in will seem incomprehensible and dangerous. Learning new rules — or having to survive in situations where there seem to be *no* rules — can be a matter of life and death.

If your characters aren't human, they will have different rules, too. The rabbits of Richard Adams's novel **Watership Down** are weak compared to their many predators, and are prone to a mental state they call "tharn" — an overwhelming fear or panic which results in them freezing on the spot. (Adams invents more general rules, too: different types of animals in his novel can understand one another's speech, as they can't in our world.) In **Watership Down**, the rabbits' world — Adams' story-world — is evoked for readers through the rules we have to learn at the start of the novel.

Think about the rules of your story world. It's likely that, even if you picked your world instinctively, its rules embody, to some degree, the values of the story you're telling: the depths of space highlight the difficulties of human survival (**Alien**), or of isolation (**Gravity**); the drawing-rooms of Jane Austen's England provide the means of social connection as well as the dangers of social ostracism or mockery; and so on.

The only rule with rules is to let the reader know them right from the start. This allows them to appreciate the main character's situation, and to anticipate how things are going to turn out. Often, it's the rules that give shape to a story, so it will not *work* as a story until those rules have been laid out.

Plot

The Turn

The most basic story element of all is: *something meaningful happens*.

It could be big, it could be small, but *something* has to happen, and it has to be *meaningful*.

A good way to think of this is a tennis match. In a game of tennis, there will always be things happening: someone in the audience sneezes, a bird flies overhead, a cloud passes over the sun, the umpire coughs. But none of these things *means* anything, because a tennis match isn't about coughs, sneezes, birds or clouds. It's about who's winning the game. So, we're only interested in who's-winning-the-game things: how well a player serves, whether the opposing player returns the ball, who misses, who hits, who stumbles, and does the ball go out of play. These are the *meaningful things* in a game of tennis.

And there are degrees of meaning. Someone scoring a point is pretty interesting; someone winning a game is more interesting; someone winning a set is even more interesting; and of course the most interesting thing of all is when they win the match. (Particularly if it's a tournament final.)

Each of these events starts with a question:

Who's going to win this point?

Who's going to win this game?

Who's going to win this set?

Who's going to win this match?

And with each point won, we get a little bit closer to knowing who's going to win the game; with each game won, we get a little bit closer to knowing who's going to win the set, and so on.

Stories are like this.

They're made up of little events adding up to bigger events, adding up to even bigger events, finally adding up to one massive event, which is the story as a whole.

Each event starts with a question in the reader's or viewer's mind: What's going to happen next? And leads onto another, similar question: *Now* what's going to happen next?

What are the meaningful things in your story?

The rules in tennis are pretty arbitrary. It could have been decided that a player wins a point by hitting the ball as high as possible, or as fast as possible, or by hitting it through a hole in the net, or by bouncing it as many times as they can between hits. But it was decided that, in tennis, you win a point when your opponent misses the ball. So that's what's meaningful in a game of tennis.

In your story, *you* set up what's meaningful. You make it clear to the reader early on what sort of story this is going to be: is it a "Does she catch the killer?" type of story, or is it a "Does he get the girl?" type of story. Once you've established that, once you've set up what's meaningful in your story, you know how the story moves forward:

Each step that takes your protagonist closer to catching the killer, or getting the girl/guy — *or* which moves them further away — is *meaningful*.

To be meaningful, each step has to do one or the other.

Each step has to change *how things are* in the basic situation of "catching the killer" or "getting the girl/guy". Otherwise nothing's happened. That's why we're calling the basic element of all stories — the basic *something meaningful that happens* — "the turn".

Things get better, things get worse. Either way, things *turn*, and we want to know what's going to happen *next*.

There's one important point to note in how a story differs from a tennis match. Because a tennis match is won by building up games and sets won, a moment might arrive where one player is very close to winning, and the other is far behind. To stand a chance of winning, the far-behind player has a lot of work to do.

In a story, though, it's more like there's only ever *one* point to play for. For most of it, our protagonist will feel like they're always on the edge of losing. And it will often seem as though they're only getting further and further away, until, just before their final confrontation with their antagonist, it seems as though they are about to lose everything.

And here's where it really differs from tennis: even when they're on the edge of losing everything, the protagonist of a story can still win the whole thing in one go. They make one move and it flips everything round. It's as though, in a tennis match, by winning *one* point, they flip the scores, and take on their opponent's winning position.

That's why it's called "the turn". At every stage, everything can flip. And as things go on, the flip only gets bigger, from win-a-point/lose-a-point to win-everything/lose-everything.

Acts

Stories can be divided into chunks of various sizes.

The smallest division (in movie scriptwriting, anyway) is the *beat*, which can represent a single line of dialogue, a single action, or even just a look, a reaction. It's like a single hit of the ball in tennis. Each beat feels like a definite action has been taken by a character, but not one that can stand alone.

Then we have the *scene*, which usually takes place in one location, and although it will be made up of lots of smaller actions, can usually be summed up as basically one thing: "They have a conversation", "They have a fight", "She finds the first clue", "He admits he's wrong". Each scene will usually feel as though it has changed the course of the story in a small but significant way: a character learns something or decides something, the power balance between the protagonist and the antagonist flips, a new character is introduced, an existing character leaves.

We then have the *sequence*, which is built up of a series of scenes that add up to one larger, overall action. A *chase sequence*, for instance, will be made up of a series of scenes in different locations, in some of which our protagonist will be gaining on their quarry, in others of which they'll suffer a setback, all ending with them either catching their quarry or losing them for good. Other examples of sequences: a date (meeting outside the restaurant, ordering the meal, eating, saying goodnight afterwards — or not), dealing with an emergency (air-pressure klaxons go off in the space-station, there's a rush to get into suits, a frantic search, the leak is found, then it's fixed), and so on. Not every scene has to be part of a sequence, but you'll know when they are.

The largest division (until we get to the whole story itself) is the *act*. Like the smaller story elements, an act encompasses a change in the story, but it is a *major* change. Act one: we learn there's a serial killer on the loose. Act two: more victims' bodies turn up, but our protagonist realises what connects the victims, and therefore how to catch the killer. Act three: our protagonist realises *they* are the intended next victim, and that they've been drawn into a final showdown.

The term "act" was initially used for theatrical plays. The end of an act was a curtain-down moment, a chance for the audience to take a break, stretch their legs, get a drink, go to the bathroom, and so on. This meant that an act had to end at a very specific moment. You don't, after all, want the audience drifting off, getting caught up in a conversation at the bar, or perhaps even going home. That would mean the curtain would come up on a half-empty theatre. An act has to end at a point that leaves the audience wanting more.

At the same time, you can't end in the middle of a dramatic scene — mid-fight, mid-argument, or just before a major revelation — because that would be throwing away the suspense you'd built up.

The best way to end an act is just *after* a dramatic highpoint, at the point when the protagonist has been forced into a realisation that changes the whole story. There's a natural pause, here, but one of stunned silence rather than relaxation. This means the scene's dramatic suspense has been played out, but there's still a compelling reason for the audience to come back. They want to know what happens next.

And this is a natural way for stories to work. An act begins with that new realisation sinking in. (Acts often start with a "pause for breath", a relatively quiet moment after the last act's dramatic high-point ending.) The protagonist starts pursuing a new line of intent based on what has just happened. The action builds up and up, until finally we're back in another major confrontation — the ultimate consequence of the protagonist's realisation at the end of the previous act. This confrontation plays out, and again the protagonist learns something, and has to come to another, wholly new, realisation. There's the feeling of stunned reevaluation, and the curtain comes down. (Or, in a movie, the next act starts on its quiet, "pause for breath" moment. Often there's a fade-to-black between acts.)

The exceptions to this pattern, of course, are the first and last acts.

In the first act, we won't be following on from a previous act's "new realisation". Instead, we'll see our protagonist going about their normal life, until they (pretty soon) get caught up in the story. At this point, though, they won't have taken a major decision. In the first act, the protagonist reacts to their situation as they've *always* reacted, and it's only when this fails (in the dramatic high-point at the end of act one), that they're forced to reevaluate their approach. Which sets things up for act two.

The other exception is the final act. Here, after the final confrontation, the protagonist will probably be victorious, or (if yours is a downbeat ending) they'll have lost beyond any chance of coming back. After that, instead of a moment of reevaluation, we have the point the whole story has been moving towards: a moment of clear sight, a feeling that now, at last, our character is seeing things (either themselves or the world, or perhaps both) as they truly are. They have learned the lesson of the story.

Acts, then, generally take the same basic shape:

- a (deceptively) quiet start
- an escalation of conflict
- the final dramatic-high point (the *Crisis*)
- the moment of stunned reevaluation that sets up the next act (or, in the final act, a moment of acceptance or recognition that ends the story) (the *Climax*)

One act, three acts, five acts

How many acts make up a story?

A short play, movie, or story is often a single act. It builds to a single dramatic high-point, resolves it, and ends.

Anything longer, such as a novel or feature-length movie, will usually be built up of more than one act. Three acts is often described as the "classic" structure. Read enough movie reviews, and you're bound to come across the phrase, "It has a classic three-act structure". Five acts is another.

Why three? Why five?

The answer to this may be down to the fundamental way we have said that stories work: they're all about *the turn*. A turn means the story takes a flip. At the start of a story, let's say, things are going well for the protagonist, or at least they're "normal". Then, at the end of the first act, things flip, and now they're definitely *not* going well. It takes the end of the second act to flip them back again, and the third act to play things out to their conclusion. If you add more acts, you'll have to add them in pairs so they flip *away* and back *again*.

Another take on it is that three, in story terms, is a magic number. In fairy tales, people are often granted three wishes, or there are three sisters (Cinderella and her two ugly sisters) or three brothers (two sure-fire hits and the one nobody expects to win), or three paths to choose from, three suitors, and so on.

I like to call three the *heroic number*.

The heroic number

Think about it like this. Our protagonist decides to climb a mountain. They look at the mountain, choose the best route, go up, and get to the top.

Great. But we're left feeling they didn't really experience any difficulties. That couldn't have been a very hard mountain to climb.

So, a different take. Our protagonist decides to climb a mountain. They look at the mountain, choose what seems the best route, and start up. But they get halfway and encounter difficulties, forcing them back down. They look at the mountain again. "Aha," they think. "I see where I went wrong." They pick another route, and this time get to the top.

In other words: fail, learn, try again. That's what *most* people would do. But stories aren't about "most people".

So how about this. Our protagonist decides to climb a mountain. They look at the mountain, choose what seems the best route, and start up. They get halfway and encounter difficulties, forcing them back down. They look at the mountain again. "Aha. I see where I went wrong." They pick another route, but fail *again*. They're forced back down. "Give up, buddy!" everyone says, but no, they're determined. They look at the mountain, and pick yet another route — one that nobody would have picked first off. But they go that way, and this time they get to the top.

Now it feels our protagonist has really *earned* having their story told. They didn't have an *easy* time of it, nor did they have a *reasonable* time of it. They went beyond the bounds, beyond the point where most would have given up. But they succeeded.

This is what heroes do. And that's why three feels like the *heroic number*.

(If you have the same character take four goes to get to the top of the mountain, it doesn't add much to the story.)

So, three acts feels like we're giving our protagonist a *real test*. They don't have things easy, they don't have things reasonable. They have to go beyond the bounds.

The classic three act structure

As three acts is such a classic structure, let's look at how it usually breaks down:

Act one. The story opens, the problem is defined. This act has to do a lot. It has to grab us (the *Hook*), introduce the main characters, and lead up to the first act's Crisis (the *Inciting Incident*).

Act two. The situation complicates. This is often the longest act. It's also the darkest, as it's the one where, despite our protagonist's best efforts, it's the antagonist who seems to be winning. At some Halfway Point things change, but often, at this act's Crisis, it feels like our protagonist's darkest moment. They've lost everything, and the worst that *could* happen *has* happened.

Act three. The resolution. It's quite common, particularly in action stories, for the third act to be *one long sequence* — a major battle between the protagonist and antagonist ending in one's defeat, and the other's victory.

Acts are, in a sense, the most invisible of your story's structural elements. You *know*, in a movie, when a scene begins and ends (often, the scenery changes), but you might have to think about it for a moment, even with your favourite movie, to know when the acts change.

But if you don't think, and instead *feel* — for those moments of high dramatic tension, followed by stunned reevaluation, then the "pause for breath" as a new act starts — you'll spot them quickly.

Stories are fractal

"Fractal" is a word originally used of a certain type of mathematical pattern, and of shapes in nature, which are said to be "self-similar". This means that, if you dive into a *detail* of the shape, it starts to look the same as the overall original shape. So, for instance, the frond of a fern-leaf itself looks like a fern leaf.

Stories are also "fractal". What this means is that the *smaller* components of a story — the acts, the scenes, even the separate actions within the scenes — are, in a way, mini-stories.

If a story is about one large "turn" — one large change in the ways things are — it will be made up of a series of smaller "turns", each of which is made of still smaller "turns".

In structural terms, this means a scene within a story can be approached as if it were a separate story. It has a beginning, and an end; it has a Halfway Point where things change; and it has a Crisis at the end that forces the protagonist to make a decision that moves the story on. (These terms are explored more fully in the next section.)

If you're having a problem with a story element, be it an act or a scene or just a beat, it might help to isolate it from the larger story and think of it as a story on its own. How does it start? How does it end? What changes, where, and why? How is it shaped? Is it story-shaped? If not, can it be *made* story-shaped?

All that you learn about stories can be applied to the smaller elements of stories. Each moment will "turn", and each moment will drive the story forward, building up a tightly-linked chain of events binding your story's *beginning* to its *ending*.

Story Shape

The Hook

Every story begins with a promise

The simplest promise of all is "Once upon a time…" — the promise that what follows is a story worth telling, and worth listening to.

Generally, though, we want more than that. We, as readers or viewers, want a hint of what's to come. We want to know it's worth our while investing in this story, and what sort of story it's going to be. Is this going to be an edge-of-the-seat thriller? Or an emotional rollercoaster? Is it going to be taut and suspenseful, or full of wham-bang action? Are we going to have to attune to a character's psychological depths, or is it going to be all about spectacular visuals and wild ideas? If our main character is going to suffer, should we laugh *at* them or cry *with* them?

This is what the "Hook" is all about. Its job is not just to hook our attention, but to hook us into the right frame of mind for the story. Like a fly-fisher angling for fish, you have to bait your hook with the right sort of bait.

The Hook is the first thing a story does, and though this means there can be a lot riding on it (if it goes wrong, you may lose your audience or readership right from the start), you also have a lot of leeway. The Hook doesn't have to be full of meaning and significance, it just has to lay out the basic promise of the story by saying — or, better still, *showing* — what sort of story it's going to be.

For an action-adventure story, particularly with a series character who has a lot of similar adventures, the Hook can be an almost separate mini-adventure (or the end stages of one). The James Bond movies were the first to use this approach, and the Indiana Jones movies took it on quite naturally. Think of the start of **Raiders of the Lost Ark**, where we see Indy at the end of what has obviously been a long quest to find this temple in the jungle. He goes in, avoiding or second-guessing traps, and comes out with the treasure — only to have it taken from him. This section could be removed from the movie without altering the story (apart from the fact that the villain in this opening section returns, but Indy's reaction to him would be enough to tell us they're old enemies). But what this Hook section does is play out the story that's to come, in miniature: it's full of ingenious traps and dangerous pitfalls, betrayals and greedy villains, with a golden treasure at the heart of it (which, as in the movie that follows, gets taken away from Indy once he's done all the hard work). By the end of the Hook we know we're going to be in for a real thrill ride of a movie with a tough, likeable, often-lucky-but-not-always hero. (With the added bonus that, with all those thrills, the movie has bought itself a little quiet time to set up the main story with some less actionful exposition scenes.)

In some cases, the setting itself can be a Hook. This is particularly true of science fiction, where the setting — a dystopian future, a harsh alien planet, the depths of space — defines a lot of what the story is going to be about. Just having a lone character on Mars is enough to tell us that this story will be about surviving in an inhospitable environment millions of miles from help. A science fiction story based around a single aspect of technology — one where law-enforcers can predict crimes before they happen, for instance, or where people can have old, unwanted or boring memories replaced by exciting new ones — will need to lay this out right at the start by demonstrating it.

(An exception to this, of course, is where the story is going to lead to some revelation about the true nature of this world, as in **The Matrix**, which has to lead us up to Neo learning that the world he moves through every day is an illusion. Here, though, the Hook's job is to give us a hint that *something* is wrong with reality.)

If your world has rules (see Rules), they will probably be laid out in the Hook — and that may be *all* the Hook has to do, if your world's rules are the basis of your story. But most likely, you'll also want to give them your story's special spin. If this is a story in a world where people can have their memories replaced, is it a love story (**Eternal Sunshine of the Spotless Mind**) or an action adventure story (**Total Recall**)? The Hook has to let the readers know.

Although voice-over narration in movies is often frowned on, there are cases where this approach works as a Hook. Fantasy stories set in invented lands often use this technique. Movies like **Conan the Barbarian** and **The Lord of the Rings** set up the story that follows by telling us the basic facts about this new, magical land we're about to visit. Fantasy novels often do this, too. Every book of David Eddings's **Belgariad** series begins with a short retelling of a myth or legend from its invented land.

Stories set in historical periods can do something similar. Sometimes, just presenting a date is enough, as with any year in the midst of either World War. This is enough to start getting readers or audience into the right frame of mind for the story that is to follow.

If your story is all about unfolding a mystery, you'll have to be careful with how much you reveal in your Hook, but you should at least reveal what *sort of* mystery it is, or keep to the same *type* of story. **Psycho**, for example, whose director Alfred Hitchcock very much wanted audiences *not* to be prepared for what was going to happen halfway through the movie, opens without any hint of its titular psychopath, but it does soon get underway with a crime story. Besides, what Hitchcock wanted was to get his audience invested in the opening character played by Janet Leigh, so his intent was to draw us into her life, her narrative. (By this time in his career, Hitchcock's very name was a sort of Hook — people would come to see his movies because they were by him. The name "Hitchcock" was already a promise of the sort of movie that would follow.)

In less action-oriented stories, the Hook could be about presenting us with a key aspect of the main character's emotional life. One common technique for this is to show us a typical event from their life, with the feeling that this *is* typical — another bad date, another break-up phone call, another tough day at work, or a good day at work that ends with a return to an empty home. All showing us what is wrong with this character's life, and which will have to be fixed, or at least faced, in the story to come.

When coming up with a Hook, think about the kind of story you're telling, and how you can communicate that to the reader. Think about "priming" them, letting them know what sort of emotions they're going to be engaging, or what sort of experiences they're going to be having in this book or movie. Then, if it's an emotional story, they'll be ready to open up to the characters; if it's an action story, they'll be ready for thrills; if it's a horror story, they'll be primed with the sort of scares to expect.

Think of the Hook as the distant rumble in the sky that tells you a storm's on its way.

Then you can bring on the lightning.

The Inciting Incident

Although your story will probably begin with a Hook that both grabs the reader/audience *and* gives them an idea of what sort of story is going to follow, the story doesn't *really* kick off until what's often called the "Inciting Incident".

This is because there has to be a certain amount of set-up, in terms of world, character and situation, before the significance of what's going on really hits us. And the Inciting Incident is the point where the story *really gets going* — where the character and world and what is to happen click into place. Up till now, the race cars have been revving at the starting line; *this* is when the flag goes down and the race begins.

It's also the point at which our main character makes their first major *decision*, and takes their first important *action*.

It's true that people are constantly making decisions and taking actions every moment of their lives. But a lot of those will be minor decisions, or things that follow on from what they've done before, or things someone else has told them to do. The Inciting Incident is something *new* for them, something challenging and perhaps frightening but also engaging. It comes to the main character as a chance to show their true mettle, by bringing out something that's uniquely them. Up to now, anyone could have been doing what they were doing. This is where we see why *this* is the character we're following.

Think of the opening to **The Silence of the Lambs**. The Hook here is mostly about situation. We're introduced to

Clarice Starling, a small and not physically imposing woman in a world that seems full of tall, physically imposing men. We can see that she's determined, but we can also see that she has a lot to go up against. And this is only further underlined when, asked to wait in Jack Crawford's office, she's confronted by a wall of photographs of a murdered woman. This is the only other woman we've seen so far in the movie, and she's a victim. Starling then meets Crawford who tells her she's to interview the notorious serial killer Hannibal Lecter. She goes to the institute where Lecter is held and meets another man-in-charge, who again starts telling her what to do. Finally, she gets in front of Lecter, and she's alone with one of the most evil men in the world. This, we feel, is where things are really going to get going. This is the story's Inciting Incident.

It's also here that Clarice takes her first truly decisive action and shows her true strength as a character, a strength that all those hulking men back at the FBI don't have. Faced with this evil man who is clearly enjoying playing games with her, Clarice decides not to try to outwit or impress him, but to be honest with him. She answers his questions not with throwaway or evasive responses but by being genuine, and this is what — after a lot of testing — gets her a result. Lecter gives her not an outright answer, but at least *a clue*.

Up until this point, Clarice has been doing what she's been told to do. Now she's doing what *she* has decided to do. And we feel, watching this scene, that she gets her results because of *who she is*. Not just because she interviewed Lecter (she was *told* to do that) but because of *how* she did it.

In the Inciting Incident, there's often a feeling, after the main character's first decisive action, that, although it *is* showing their genuine character, it is perhaps just their standard response to a situation, or not their best response.

After all, this is still the beginning of the story and our character has a lot to learn. But we, as readers or audience, get to see what it is the main character has to learn from their response to the Inciting Incident.

For instance, the main character of Jane Austen's **Emma**, Emma Woodhouse, is a clever young woman who, a little too sure of her own cleverness, decides she's very good at matchmaking among her friends and acquaintances. When she gets a new friend, Harriet Smith, she immediately sets about reshaping her — telling her how to dress and how to act — all in preparation for finding her a husband of Emma's choosing, not Harriet's. Her first act is to convince Harriet not to marry the vicar, Mr Elton, even though he would be a good match, because Emma wants something better for *her* Harriet.

This is Emma Woodhouse's first decisive action in our eyes as readers and viewers (it's a novel that's been adapted several times, including a modern take in the movie **Clueless**). We can see that Emma *means* well — she wants to improve Harriet's lot in life — but we can also see she's interfering in matters of the heart where she ought not to interfere, and where *cleverness* should give way to *feeling*, not the other way round. We can sense, at this point, that although Emma succeeds in her intention of persuading Harriet *not* to marry Mr Elton, the story that follows is going to give young Emma Woodhouse a well-deserved (but ultimately kind) lesson about interfering too much in other people's love lives — as well as, of course, opening up her own.

The Inciting Incident is rarely the opening to the story, but is usually the first point at which we feel things really *get going*, that it's time to settle down into our seats and get stuck into the story. We've had the appetiser (the Hook), now it's time for the main meal.

The Halfway Point

At its most basic, a story is about a "turn" — about things changing from one state to another. And as with all change, there comes a point where things have gone too far to back out from or undo. By this point, the protagonist will be *committed*, whether they like it or not. This is the tipping point, the "I love you" moment, the "now it's personal" moment.

It's often a high point for the protagonist. Things seem to be going really well. They might even feel as though they've attained their goal. But it's also at this point, as soon as the protagonist reaches that stage of total commitment, that the forces against them — the baddies, the monster, the disapproval of their peers, the unjust laws of their time — ramp things up and show what they're truly capable of.

Almost always, this happens at a story's Halfway Point.

Let's examine some Halfway Points to see how this works.

At the Halfway Point in Shakespeare's **Romeo and Juliet**, the "star-cross'd lovers" have just married in secret. This seems like the fulfilment of all their hopes and desires, a high point in their lives. But what happens next? A fight breaks out between their two families, and Romeo gets involved in it, killing Tybalt, his new wife's cousin. As a result, he's exiled from his and Juliet's home city of Verona. No sooner has he united with Juliet in marriage than he's separated from her, on pain of death.

In **Ghostbusters**, the Halfway Point sees things ramp up

on two levels. Just prior to the Halfway Point, everything seems to be going well for the team, as they're getting famous, and earning a living at last. Even better, Bill Murray's character Dr Venkman is set to go on a date with Sigourney Weaver's Dana Barrett. But what happens? Dana is suddenly possessed by a supernatural power and becomes "the Gatekeeper", the first stage in the return of the world-destroying god Zuul. Not only does this mean that what the Ghostbusters are up against has ramped up from a series of individual spooks to a major, world-ending god-like power, but it's also directly affecting Venkman's love-interest: now, it's personal.

The Halfway Point is when the protagonist is forced to realise exactly what they're up against. In **Back to the Future**, the Halfway Point comes when Marty sees, for the first time, just how complicated his trip into the past has made things: "Wait a minute, Doc. Are you trying to tell me that my mother… has the *hots* for me?" Not only does he have to get himself back to his own time, he also has to arrange it so his hopeless father and his hots-for-him mother get together. At this point, he seems further than ever from getting home.

Often, it's at the Halfway Point that we get a movie's most well-known scene.

What's the Halfway Point in **Psycho**? The shower scene. Before that, the movie was Janet Leigh's character's story; now it's all about Norman Bates.

What's the Halfway Point in **Alien**? The chestbuster scene. Just before that, John Hurt's Kane seemed to have recovered from the alien facehugger's attack, and the crew were all looking forward to going back into their stasis units for the trip back to Earth. Afterwards, they know they've got a predatory alien on board the ship, and they won't be going to sleep till they've dealt with it.

The Halfway Point can seem to change the whole world

of the story, or at least the rules by which it operates.

In **Jurassic Park**, the Halfway Point is the T. Rex attack. From that point on, Jurassic Park is no longer an amusement park for humans, it's a hunting ground for dinosaurs.

In Umberto Eco's medieval murder-mystery novel **The Name of the Rose** (and the movie based on it), the Halfway Point is when the Inquisition turn up. Before that, the investigation into who was murdering monks at the abbey was in the hands of the rational and reasonable Brother Baskerville (Sean Connery); now, it's in the hands of the intolerant, witch-burning Inquisitor Bernardo Gui, who will get the confessions *he* wants, and not necessarily the truth. (And Gui also happens to be Brother Baskerville's longstanding rival, so, again, "now, it's personal".)

There's usually a feeling, from the Halfway Point onwards, of downhill acceleration towards the Climax of the final act, and so of the story as a whole. This is the tipping point, the moment when things really start to ramp up.

Next time you're watching a movie, keep an eye on the running time. As things get close to halfway, watch out for this halfway tipping point, and see how it changes (often subtly, but decisively) the whole feel of the movie.

Crisis

A Crisis is a *decision point* in a story. (The word "crisis" ultimately derives from the Ancient Greek word for "decision".) But we're not talking about the point at which the main character, asked if they want a coffee, has to decide if they want it black-with-sugar or white-without. Crisis points are *meaningful* decisions. And often, they are the points where something forces the protagonist to make a decision they wouldn't willingly make.

These are the real turning points in a story. In fact, Crisis points usually arrive at the end of each act. Throughout the act, we feel as though we're heading towards a point where a difficult decision *has* to be made, and the Crisis occurs when that point can no longer be put off.

We've already encountered the idea that the Inciting Incident, which kicks off the real body of a story, occurs when the protagonist is forced to make their *first real decision*. This is a Crisis point. The Inciting Incident usually happens at the end of a story's first act.

But what follows are a series of decisions, each of which leads to the protagonist being forced to make *another* decision, usually as a result of a previous decision being not *quite* right, until, at the very end, they finally make the *right* decision — though one they'd never have had the nerve, strength, or self-knowledge to make at the start.

In a way, a story could be said to be about a *chain* of decisions a protagonist makes, each of which doesn't quite go right, until the final decision, which *does*.

Comedy makes this obvious. In **Planes, Trains and**

Automobiles, Steve Martin's character, Neal Page, is trying to get home for Thanksgiving, and first of all has to get to the airport. Finding himself pressed for time and unable to flag down a taxi, he makes his first decision, to *pay* someone who *has* just flagged down a taxi to let him have it. While he's paying them, though, Del Griffith (played by John Candy) gets into the taxi and takes off. Neal's first decisive act went spectacularly wrong. But, in story terms, it introduced us to Del Griffith and the effect he's going to have on Neal Page's life.

Neal gets to the airport, where he bumps into Del again, and even finds himself sitting next to him on the plane. Then the story throws another obstacle in his way: bad weather forces the plane to be diverted to Wichita. Finding himself in a strange city without a hotel booking, Neal is forced to make another decision: spend a night without a bed, or take up this annoying man Del's offer of a shared hotel room. It's hard, but Neal decides to be sensible and takes the room. And the upshot of *that* decision is a night of arguments, *plus* the pair have their wallets stolen. *Now* what are they going to do?

This being comedy, it could be said that the point is, *no* decision Neal makes will *ever* go right. Each time, he's forced, against his will, to pair up with Del, and each time it goes wrong. After all, if it didn't, there wouldn't be a comedy. But the illusion that, at each stage, Neal *has* a choice is what makes it all the more aggravating for him, and hilarious for us.

Consider Luke's story in the first **Star Wars** movie, **A New Hope**. When he finds his new R2 unit playing part of a hologram message, Luke *decides* to remove the droid's restraining bolt so it can play the whole message. The upshot is, though, that he doesn't get to see the message, and R2-D2 escapes.

Luke *decides* to go after him with C-3PO, and they find

the rogue droid, but they're vulnerable out here in the desert, and Luke is attacked by Sand People. After being saved by Old Ben Kenobi, and seeing the whole of the hologram message, Luke is offered the chance of leaving his home planet of Tatooine and joining the Rebellion. He *decides* not to, but when he gets home, he finds his Aunt and Uncle killed by Imperial Stormtroopers. It seems like he has no choice after all.

At each stage, each decision Luke makes isn't quite right, but it does drive the story forward. His final decision, though, is the one that pays off. Attacking the Death Star at the end of the movie, Luke *decides* (prompted by the disembodied voice of Obi Wan Kenobi) to turn off his battle computer, and judge for himself when to fire his torpedoes. This, at last, is the moment when things go spectacularly right.

At every stage in a story, the protagonists will be faced with decisions, often ones they are forced into — and then they're faced with the *outcome* of that decision, which demands *another* decision. A story could be described as a series of answers to the question, "What do they decide to *do*?" followed by "And what happens because of *that*?" Over and over again, till the end: "*Then* what do they decide to do? And what happens because of *that*?"

This constant progression gives a story its momentum, moving it through scenes and acts, ramping up the pressure at every stage. There's a feeling of inescapability, as each action or decision requires *another* action or decision, and then *another*, and *another*, with the stakes rising at each step, until, finally, we reach the end.

Climax

The Climax is the moment when the promise of all the dramatic tension built up in a scene, act, or story as a whole, is delivered.

In all but one case (the final Climax, that ends the story), the Climax won't resolve *everything*, but will instead open up new complications that have to be answered in the following scenes. This is how a story progresses, with each scene ending on a moment that drives the story into the *next* scene, and each act ending on a twist or revelation that drives the story into the *next* act.

The exception, of course, is the final Climax, in which everything that *can* be resolved *is* resolved. The villain is defeated, the lovers are united, the hero's efforts are finally recognised. (Or, if your story is making a point about how things "really are", you might have the villain win, the lovers split for good, and so on. Either way, it has to be an end of things.)

The Obligatory Scene

Robert McKee, in his book **Story**, puts forward the idea of there being, in every story, an "Obligatory Scene". This is a scene at the end of a story that balances the Inciting Incident which occurred at the beginning. If you think of the Inciting Incident as asking a question ("Will she win?", "Will he get the girl?", "Will they find the lost dog?"), the

Obligatory Scene is your story's *answer* to that question.

And this is the point about stories. A story starts with what is, essentially, a *promise*. The writer presents their readership or audience with a character, a situation, a world, in which something is *not right*. There's a tension that needs to be resolved. And the readership or audience sticks with the story because they want to see the writer *take things to the fulfilment of that promise*: they want things to be *made right*, or, if not right, they want something important or valuable or true to be said about why things *cannot* be made right.

This promise is fulfilled in the story's Climax. This is the point at which the story *says* what it's *saying* (see the section on Story Value for more on this). This is the point at which the readers or viewers should feel that everything that *can* be resolved (allowing for the messiness of life) *has* been resolved — and, if possible, resolved in an interesting way.

Endings

One of my favourite resolutions to any story is in John Grisham's **The Firm** (and the movie based on it). I'm not going to give away the ending, but the story is about a young and idealistic lawyer taken on by a small but high-powered law firm, who turn out to be secretly representing the Mob. Our protagonist is approached by the FBI and told that he has to turn informant against his employers, or face being jailed alongside them. But if he *does* turn informant, he'll be breaking the attorney-client privilege by sharing details about his firm's clients, after which he'll no longer be able to practise law. So, he's caught in a stark dilemma, in which he either risks prison or ends the career he's been working towards all his life.

What does he do? Presented with an apparent two-choice dilemma, he uses his ingenuity and knowledge of the law to find his own, new "third way" — a clever solution that allows him to fulfil the demands of the law without having to pay its heavy price.

There's nothing you can do to stop your readers or audience from trying to guess the ending of your story. In fact, it can be one of the pleasures of being told a story, to try to work out how things will end. The only thing to avoid is disappointing them by not fulfilling their *expectations* about the *kind* of ending they get. If all they're expecting at the end is a massive explosion, it's easy to fulfil that expectation. If, however, you've led them to expect a "clever" ending — if your story has been full of twists and turns, plots and counterplots, and so on — then you have to provide just that.

Endings could be said to divide into three types:

- **Happily-ever-after** — Everything is tied up neatly, every plot strand is resolved, and each character gets what they deserve. This is often the case in comedies, where everyone is married or paired off at the end, except for the villain who gets their (comic) comeuppance. It's also true of straightforwardly heroic tales, where the "goodies" win and "baddies" lose. There's a heartwarming and affirmative feeling to this sort of ending, as this is how we *want* things to be.

- **Bittersweet** — Things mostly end well, but there's a balancing note of things not being perfect. This can add depth and realism to a story, making it feel more convincing and true. This sort of ending is how we feel things generally *are*.

- **Downbeat** — Things end negatively, or ambiguously, often with a pessimistic feeling that "this is how things are in the *real* world". Such an ending can make a powerful negative statement, but can leave readers or viewers who just wanted a little escapism feeling betrayed, if they're not properly prepared for it. (Though, of course, you may *want* to shock them in this way.) This sort of ending is how we *fear* things really are.

Think about what sort of ending you're setting your audience or readership up for in your story. If possible, think how you might add a little twist to it to take it that one stage further than your audience is expecting. But also consider the *style* of ending they have been led to expect: happily-ever-after, bittersweet, or downbeat? It can be a delicate balancing act, but as the ending is the thing your readers or audience walk away with, it's worth taking the time to get right.

Story Meaning

Story Value

Stories work, ultimately, by being about *one meaningful thing*.

We know, from the Inciting Incident on, what final situation the story is moving towards: the world is saved, the killer is caught, the couple is united, the lost puppy is found. And the story will only work if this final situation is *meaningful*, otherwise why would a reader or viewer stick with it through all the tension, suspense, and heartache on the way?

This doesn't mean every story has to be about saving the world, of course. Stories can take the smallest things and make them meaningful; often, they're about saving one person, not a whole world — not that this is in any way a small thing.

What's far more important is that a story is, ultimately and overall, about *one* meaningful thing. Other aspects of life can, and will, be brought in, but a story works best when it has one, clear source of meaning throughout.

This is what we call the *Story Value*.

It can be something primal, like *survival*, either of an individual, a group, or a whole world. In **Alien** and its sequels, for instance, the value is clearly survival. As the first movie starts, Ripley and her fellow crew members are already in a precarious situation — they are human beings travelling through the vacuum of space, an environment that's hostile to human beings. Then the alien creature turns up and things get much, much worse. The creature is, in story terms, *perfectly designed* to test Ripley's ability to *survive*: we know almost nothing about it other than it is very, very good at killing people, and that's what it wants to do. **Alien** takes its Story Value of survival and turns the dial up as far as it can go.

In Jane Austen's novels, a marriage based on *the love between equals* is the primary Story Value, particularly when, in her world, there are so many other pressing reasons for young women to marry (to be saved from poverty, for instance; or to gain in social standing). In Jane Austen's novels, a marriage that brings together two people of equal intelligence, wit, and character wins through in the end, though only after other temptations (marriage for security's sake, or marriage to a flashily handsome but empty man) have been put in her characters' paths and been resisted.

Whatever the central Story Value is, stories say something fundamental about human nature. It's this, ultimately, that speaks to us as readers and viewers as we go through a story, however much we're involved in the action and characters on a moment-by-moment basis. A story's *Story Value* is what makes it feel true, and meaningful.

This doesn't mean that, as a writer, you have to point it out at every stage. Quite the opposite. Once it's set up as your story's value (and it should be felt right at the start, as part of your Hook), your readers and viewers will be looking for it, perhaps unconsciously, in every scene. It has to be quietly but intimately involved in every story turn. There's almost never going to be a point where it has to be stated outright, but if it's ever absent, your readers and viewers will notice, and perhaps start to feel that something was missing in that last scene…

Once you know what value lies behind your story, keep it in mind. Think about it. Feel its importance to you, and your characters, and its presence in your story. It should be there in every scene, it should drive every turn, and it should be the thing that is won or lost as the story comes to an end. It's what's *at stake*. It's what, with your story, you are *saying*.

The Vice

One way Story Value makes itself felt in a story is by being held up against its *opposite* value.

Against *survival*, obviously, we have *death*.

Against the *marriage of equals*, we have the possibility of being trapped in a *marriage based on pretence*, and only ever growing more and more hollow.

If you know your Story Value, it should be easy to find its opposite. Justice — injustice. Freedom — oppression. Acceptance — rejection.

In some cases, you might need to think about what particular opposite value you are choosing. Against *love*, you might have *hate*, for instance, but you also might have *lovelessness*, or *isolation*. Against *being trapped*, you might have *freedom*, but you might also have *belonging*.

Ultimately, this clash of opposite values is what your story will be moving towards, but it won't be laid out like that at the beginning. At the start, your protagonist will be faced by a lesser version of this clash of fundamental values. As the story moves forwards, this clash will only get more compelling, more desperate, and harder to escape from.

Like being caught in a vice.

Stories rarely start by throwing their protagonist right in against the ultimate threat, the complete opposite of their Story Value. In part, this is because a story has to have somewhere to go. Unless your story really is going to be nothing but a fight from beginning to end (in which case it's surely wrong to call it a *story*), there will have to be some progression in the forces your protagonist is up against.

This has several beneficial effects: by building up the strength and difficulty of what your protagonist is facing, your readers or viewers get to properly appreciate that your protagonist really is up against something serious, and it also makes us feel (through seeing how your protagonist is tested, how they learn, and better themselves) that your protagonist has truly *earned* their victory at the end.

Because of this, you can usually map out your story as having your main character or characters being faced with a *series* of threats that only get worse and worse, or stronger and stronger, as the story goes on. In addition, each time your protagonist overcomes one threat and finds themselves facing another, they'll probably find themselves with more to lose.

Let's look at how this works in our earlier Story Value example, the movie **Alien**. At the start, the crew of the spaceship Nostromo aren't heroes. They're normal people, whose only interest is doing their jobs, getting back to Earth, and getting paid. Although there's a danger to their lives (they're in a spaceship far from Earth, and therefore far from rescue) it's not an immediate danger. The first level of threat comes when they find they've been woken from stasis not because they're almost home but because the ship's computer has detected a signal coming from a nearby planet and it has to be investigated. Quite naturally, some of the crew refuse — till they're told that this situation is in their contract, and if they don't do it, they'll lose all shares in the current operation.

So, at this stage, there's a threat, but it's not a threat to life. The most they might lose is some money.

Landing on the planet, they're exposed to a slightly higher level of environmental risk, as the landing wasn't smooth and their craft needs repair. At this stage, there's a possibility they might never get off the planet. But repairs seem to be in hand, so it's not a high risk.

Then one of their number is attacked by an alien organism. This is bad, but it's only one of them, and the organism seems to be dead. The risk (as far as Ripley is concerned) is that they all might get infected, but nobody except her takes this seriously.

Things continue to ramp up when the crew get back up into space and things actually look like returning to normal. They're all taking one final meal before going back into stasis and snoozing their way back to Earth. Then the worst happens: the alien organism wasn't dead, but was incubating inside Kane, and now it comes out in the most bloody and spectacular way.

Still, the risk isn't terrible. The crew know there's an alien on board, and they know they'll have to deal with it before going to sleep again. But surely a crew of six can deal with one snake-sized creature…

But, it turns out, it's not snake-sized anymore. It has grown, and it kills again. From now on, there's an increasingly desperate battle to destroy this creature by any means possible simply to *survive*. Nobody is worried about shares, contracts, or pay, anymore. In fact, they're quite willing to blow up the ship — precious cargo and all — just to get free of this one, deadly creature.

You can see that, although the Story Value of *survival* is present from the start, it comes more and more to the fore as the story progresses. It also becomes more and more pressing. At the start, the threat to the crew's survival is *passive* — it's the harsh environment of space that might kill them, but they're in a big spaceship and this is obviously not a pioneering voyage, it's run-of-the-mill, with tried and tested technology. But by the end, the danger is very much *not* passive — in fact, it's as aggressive as it gets. It's a big monster with two sets of teeth and acid for blood.

This feeling of things closing in on the main characters is the *Story Vice*. As the dangers increase, so do the stakes (what the characters stand to lose). Finally, the characters are caught between losing everything or winning once and for all, with no other way out.

Alien is, obviously, a dramatic example, but the same vice-like effect, though on a quieter level, occurs in stories where the stakes are personal and emotional. Take, for instance, one of the love story strands in Jane Austen's **Sense and Sensibility**. Elinor Dashwood is self-effacing and reserved (the "Sense" opposed to her more passionate sister's "Sensibility"), and when she meets Edward Ferrars, who has a similar personality, the two begin to form a relationship, in their own quiet way. But it has not yet reached an "understanding" — that is, nothing has been stated explicitly between this reticent pair — before Edward's sister steps in and hastily arranges for him to be sent away to London. And, because Elinor is not the sort to put herself forward, she accepts this passively, if disappointedly. But she still has hopes.

At this stage, all that stands between them is *physical distance*. Edward is in London, Elinor and her family are moving to Devonshire. Marriage is still possible.

But soon, the Story Vice tightens further. Elinor meets Lucy Steele, who reveals, in confidence, that she and Edward have been secretly engaged for years. It's not just distance, now, that stands between Elinor and Edward, but a *longstanding engagement*. Elinor, though tortured by having to listen to Lucy's constant chatter about this engagement, is forced by the social rules of the time to accept that this is how things are. Nevertheless we, as readers, feel (and hope) that everything *could* still change. Engagements, after all, can be broken off.

Then, later in the novel, news arrives that Lucy and a Mr Ferrars have married, and it feels that Elinor will never be united with the man she loves.

The plot has one more twist in store, but it's already easy to see how Elinor's relationship with Edward — her clear equal in intellect, wit, and personality — has a series of increasingly difficult hurdles placed between it and fulfilment: first the couple are physically separated, then it turns out Edward is already promised elsewhere, and then it seems he might have actually married.

When things finally do resolve, it feels almost magical, and mainly because this ramping up of opposition has created a feeling that any sort of happy resolution would, by now, be impossible. If the two had simply married at the start, it wouldn't have got even close to the feeling Jane Austen achieves through this vice-like effect of opposing Story Values.

Story Types

You've probably heard people say that there are only seven basic types of story, or five basic types of story, or three basic types, or even that there's really only one type of story.

Christopher Booker, in his take on the subject, **The Seven Basic Plots**, identified these:

- "Overcoming the Monster"
- "Rags to Riches"
- "The Quest"
- "Voyage & Return"
- "Comedy"
- "Tragedy"
- "Rebirth"

Already you can see the difficulty. Where do love stories fit into this scheme of things? If what stands between the central couple is a forbidding parent, it might be "Overcoming the Monster". If what prevents the couple from setting up home together is lack of money, perhaps their story is "Rags to Riches". And what if one person sets out to find a person *worth* loving? Isn't that "The Quest"? And if they *come back* with that person, isn't that "Voyage & Return"? If things end happily, it might be a "Comedy", but if things end badly it could be a "Tragedy". And isn't all love, even if it doesn't work out in the end, a form of "Rebirth"?

Other people turn to fairy tales and myths to provide basic story types. A "Little Red Riding Hood" story is about an innocent character facing peril and coming through alive. A "Beauty and the Beast" story is about a seemingly monstrous character having their true, better nature seen by another, ending in that character's redemption. A "Deal with the Devil" tale is about someone trying to get something the easy way, and paying for it. And so on.

Kurt Vonnegut, in a short talk you can easily find on YouTube (just search for "Kurt Vonnegut" and "plot" and look for Kurt in front of a blackboard) said that every story could be mapped on a graph, with a line that tracks the main character's journey up and down the scale of Good versus Ill. A character might start in a low, "Ill" position (an abandoned orphan, a social outcast, a hopeless inventor), and climb to a high "Good" position by the story's end. Or they might start at a reasonably good point, a little more "Good" than "Ill" (everyday life for most people), take a dip in the middle of the story, then climb back up to where they were, or perhaps a little higher. In a classical or Shakespearean tragedy, a character might start high (as a king, or a prince, or, in modern times, a CEO or celebrity), but end low, as the result of some character flaw, or simply because of the way the world works.

Story *type* isn't the same as *genre*. Some genres, such as Romance or Crime, will come with expectations about how things will end (marriage for the couple, prison or death for the criminal), but we would still call a story by the same genre-name if it ended the opposite way (the couple agree to disagree, the criminal escapes to kill again). And some genres (such as Science Fiction) tell you nothing, really, about what's going to happen in the story, only the sort of world the story takes place in. It could be a Science Fiction love-story, a Science Fiction deal-with-the-devil, a Science Fiction Cinderella. (Though, critic and writer Brian Aldiss said that all Science Fiction basically boils down to one formula: "Hubris clobbered by Nemesis.")

Story types are *archetypes* — not fixed templates or formulas, but a bunch of ideas, associations, traditions and expectations we have about what's going to happen in a story. As a writer, you can choose to work *with* those ideas (fulfilling expectations) or *against* them (subverting expectations), to satirise or criticise, or just to present a certain point of view about how things are in the world ("love is messy", or "justice doesn't always triumph").

And it's those expectations you want to pay attention to as a writer. If you decide you're writing a "Cinderella" type of story, and set things up at the start with a main character whose virtues and positive qualities are clearly being overlooked or abused, you are also creating expectations in the reader or viewer. You can go with those expectations or against them. You can use those expectations to tease an audience and increase tension or humour. You can even use those expectations to completely deceive your readers by starting to tell one type of story, then switching to another. (As Alfred Hitchcock and Robert Bloch did in **Psycho**, which starts out as a crime caper, and ends with blood everywhere. Though that is another story type right there: "Things go badly.")

If you find yourself telling a certain type of story — however *you* choose to describe that type — it often helps to look around for other examples of the same type, to see how they work or don't work, what essential elements are involved in these types of stories, and so on. It can inspire you, get you out of a hole, and help you judge if what you're writing is saying something new. What are the current expectations? What other writers have taken things further, creating new expectations? Do you work with them, or against them?

Or, you might hate the idea that what you're writing is any sort of "type" at all, and just write it as it feels it should be. If you do, be prepared, though, that afterwards people will say, "Oh, yes, that's a classic such-and-such-type of story!"

Stories get a lot of their power through a writer playing with readers' expectations, and story type is just one way of doing that. So, use story types as you want to. Be guided by them, or inspired by them, not bound by them.

Some Story Theories & Further Reading

This book has been about the basic ideas of story structure. You'll find these ideas, or ideas like them, in many other books on screenwriting and novel writing. (Though it has to be said that books on novel writing are usually not as good at story structure as those on screenwriting. If you're a novelist, it's worth reading a how-to-write-a-screenplay book or two.)

If you're interested in learning more, here are a few suggestions for books to go deeper into learning about story structure.

Perhaps the most famous is **The Hero's Journey**. This originated in Joseph Campbell's study of the shared characteristics of various hero myths from traditional cultures throughout the world, **The Hero With A Thousand Faces**. Christopher Vogler applied these ideas to modern-day screenwriting in his book **The Hero's Journey**, coming up with twelve steps in a hero's "journey" or story:

- The Ordinary World
- The Call to Adventure
- The Refusal of the Call
- The Meeting with the Mentor
- Crossing the First Threshold
- Tests, Allies & Enemies

- The Approach to the Inmost Cave
- The Ordeal
- The Reward
- The Road Back
- Resurrection
- Return with the Elixir

It's likely you'll recognise some of these terms, as they've become widespread in the screenwriting community and beyond, in large part thanks to George Lucas's acknowledgement of Joseph Campbell's influence on the first **Star Wars** movie.

Christopher Booker's **The Seven Basic Plots** (already mentioned in the section on Story Types) is an in-depth study of what Booker sees as the seven basic types of story (which, in the end, he resolves into one single type), along with the various archetypal characters (Monsters, Light Figures, Dark Figures, and so on) we find in these stories. Although Booker breaks down each story type into a five-stage structure, his book is less intended for writers than as a general cultural study of story (the book's second half applies Booker's ideas to 20th century culture), but it can provide interesting angles on your own story, if you see it fitting into one of Booker's basic types.

Robert McKee's **Story** is something of a screenwriter's bible, with a lot of useful ideas about the structure of stories as a whole, as well as of individual acts and scenes. McKee also looks at the meaning inherent in stories, and the values they assert (justice, love, compassion, order) by their very structure. In his approach, every story has a "Controlling Idea", an assertion of a basic human value that a story focuses on, along with a *reason* for it ultimately triumphing at the end.

Some studies of the structure of stories come not from

the writing and moviemaking worlds but from academia. These approaches aren't designed for writers to make use of when coming up with stories, but if you want to explore them, there are plenty which can provide new ways of understanding or creating stories. One example is Vladimir Propp's study of Russian folktales, **The Morphology of the Folk Tale**, which identified thirty three elements that occur in such stories. In Propp's approach, not every story needed to contain each of the thirty three elements, but if they *did* occur, they always occurred in the order he identified. These elements included "Absentation" (a family member absents himself or herself from home), "Interdiction" (the main character is warned against doing something), "Violation" (the warning is ignored), and "Reconnaissance" (the villain makes an attempt at reconnaissance). In **Star Wars**, these points might be equated to:

- **Absentation** — R2-D2 wanders off in search of Obi Wan Kenobi.
- **Interdiction** — Uncle Owen says Luke can't leave the farm and pursue his dreams of being a pilot just yet.
- **Violation** — Luke leaves the farm (though only to go in search of R2-D2).
- **Reconnaissance** — Imperial forces start looking for the two missing droids and find the landed escape-pod.

And so on.

Propp's book was first published in 1928, and is not used so much by Western academics nowadays, but writers are, of course, free to pick up and use whatever works for them!

If I were to recommend one book to go deeper into ideas about story structure, it would be John Yorke's **Into the Woods**. Yorke has worked in television, on soap operas, and on both long-running and one-off dramas. His approach is to provide a basic "Roadmap of Change", based to some degree on the "five stages of grief" identified by psychiatrist Elisabeth Kübler-Ross. Yorke turns this into a map by which any sort of difficult change is effected, and so of a protagonist's journey through a story. He also looks at the fractal nature of stories, how scenes and acts can be seen as mini-stories with the same structure and flow as the main story itself, and how these chain together to provide a constant momentum in modern storytelling.

Learning about story structure needn't be like taking on a new religion. You don't have to pick one theory and stick with it. You can choose whichever one suits your current project, or pick just the elements that work for you and leave the rest. Learning about story structure is all about adding to your toolbox, not restricting your approach.

How stories work, and how they are structured, has been investigated not just by writers, but by anthropologists, psychiatrists, and academics in many fields. Stories are not just about entertainment — they are deeply linked to who we *are* as human beings. Understanding stories better will not break them, or stop them from working, any more than understanding how a symphony is structured will make it any less musical. It can only deepen our appreciation, and make the stories we create all the better for it.

Appendix

The Once Upon a Time Exercise

Whether you've finished a draft and are looking to knock your novel/script's story into better shape, or haven't started writing yet and have some ideas but not the whole plot, this is a fun and useful exercise for getting to know your story better, or just exploring where it might go.

What you do is write a brief version of your story, as if it were an old-fashioned fairy tale, using the following rules:

1. Begin with the words "Once there was a…" (character) or "Once, in a…" (setting). If your story is historical, you might use "Back in the days of…"

2. Don't name any of your characters. Call them by a description, such as "the crotchety old man", "the handsome young man", "the honest cop", "the unhappy wife", "the father", "the mother", and so on.

Aim to write a page or two, perhaps three, no more. Keep things brisk, as if you were telling the story to a child who, though interested, is likely to get bored if you slow down. Minimise detail, maximise action and event.

Also, rule three:

3. Enjoy it.

Writing your story like this brings its story qualities to the fore. You get to really see how one event kicks off another, where your main characters are facing decisions or just going with the flow of events, and where the high points are.

If you haven't yet worked out your whole plot, it's also an excellent way to try different ideas out.

(Also, if you're submitting a novel to an agent, or need to provide a short, treatment-style version of your script, you now have a pretty good starting point.)

Bibliography

Aldiss, Brian, & Wingrove, David — **Trillion Year Spree: The History of Science Fiction** (1986)

Booker, Christopher — **The Seven Basic Plots: Why We Tell Stories** (2004)

Bradley, A C — **Shakespearean Tragedy** (1904)

Campbell, Joseph — **The Hero With a Thousand Faces** (1949)

Egri, Lajos — **The Art of Dramatic Writing** (1946)

Forster, E M — **Aspects of the Novel** (1927)

Frensham, Raymond G — **Teach Yourself Screenwriting** (1996)

Gleick, James — **Chaos** (1987)

Jung, C G (editor) — **Man and His Symbols** (1964)

McKee, Robert — **Story: Substance, Structure, Style and the Principles of Screenwriting** (1997)

Poundstone, William — **Prisoner's Dilemma: John Von Neumann, Game Theory and the Puzzle of the Bomb** (1993)

Stein, Sol — **Stein on Writing** (1995)

Vogler, Christopher — **The Writer's Journey: Mythic Structure for Storytellers and Screenwriters** (1992)

Wilhelm, Kate — **Storyteller** (2005)

Yagoda, Ben — **The Sound on the Page** (2004)

Yorke, John — **Into the Woods: A Five-Act Journey Into Story** (2013)

About the Author

Murray Ewing is a writer, illustrator, musician and publisher, born in Reading in the United Kingdom. He studied Computer Science at the University of Kent, Canterbury (in the days when there was a single, brief lecture course on a thing called "hypertext mark-up language", but not yet a worldwide web to use it on).

He has published two novels, **The Fantasy Reader** and **Hello World**, a short, humorous self-help book, **Yes, You ARE A Monster!**, and has had stories published in **Dark Horizons**, **Andromeda Spaceways Inflight Magazine**, **Cyäegha**, **Saccade**, **Cosmorama**, and the British Fantasy Society's 40th anniversary anthology, **Full Fathom Forty**.

Murray wrote reviews for the pioneering webzine **Cybernet2000**, and has run his own book and film review blog since 2006. Since 1998 he has run **The Violet Apple.org.uk**, a website dedicated to the early-20th century fantasy writer David Lindsay, and has written about Lindsay in **Wormwood** and **Around the Outsider: Essays Presented to Colin Wilson on the Occasion of his 80th Birthday**.

Murray loves reading well-written and meaningful fantasy and supernatural horror novels, and lives in the South East of England.

www.ingramcontent.com/pod-product-compliance
Lightning Source LLC
Chambersburg PA
CBHW071910070526
44583CB00016B/1921